JESUS OF THE EAST

Discussion Guide

JESUS OF THE EAST

Discussion Guide
Questions, Practices, and Resources

한

Phuc Luu

Kate Martin Williams

Jessica Cole

Lily Wulfemeyer

ISBN 978-0-578-79572-0

Jesus of the East Discussion Guide: Questions, Practices, and Resources
Published by marginalia
© Copyright 2020
Phuc Luu
Kate Martin Williams
Jessica Cole
Lily Wulfemeyer

Houston, TX

Jesus of the East: Reclaiming the Gospel for the Wounded
© Copyright Herald Press 2020

For additional information about Phuc Luu's work and projects,
please visit his author site at www.phucluu.com.

CONTENTS

Reclaiming the Gospel for the Wounded

This guide is intended to be used with *Jesus of the East: Reclaiming the Gospel for the Wounded* in order to lead readers through a discussion of the book's contents. Within these pages are Questions, Practices, and Resources to deepen understanding and spark dialogue.

Luu began writing *Jesus of the East* because Christendom in the West has been eroding. Eroding, to put it baldly, because people who find themselves on the receiving end of hurt can no longer tolerate it. Dominant interpretations of Christianity have historically favored the perspectives of sinners—or, in the parlance of this book, the perpetrators of *han* 한—while further disenfranchising and disempowering victims of intimidation, prejudice, and violence. Used as an instrument wielded by the most powerful, Christianity has often become non-inclusive, and is sometimes even weaponized against the most vulnerable.

In contrast, Jesus saw the deep hurt among his people—those who were the poor, the demonized, the sick, the laborers, who were othered as the so called "sinners" of his society—and sought to bring healing to their deep hurt. His observation was that, without the restoration of their humanity, hurt would fester and turn into violence. Jesus saw this in the violent insurrectionists who sought to overthrow Roman power. He also saw this in the violence committed by his own people onto others in his community. Jesus came to be a physician of the sick, and those who could admit their sickness could find the healing they were seeking.

More than ever, we are seeing the glaring injustices of Western society prominently displayed on our screens and as we go about our daily lives. If people continue to operate out of denial and defensiveness, problems will not disappear. Rather, the crises of our time will be exacerbated. Many of those who are privileged to not be directly affected are either digging their heels into old fear-driven rubrics, or are bravely becoming allies. Either way, with the onslaught of injustices exposed daily, or hourly, hiding out is neither prudent nor possible.

The deaths of Breonna Taylor, Ahmaud Arbery, and George Floyd this year have sparked national protests. The continual use of the racist monikers "Chinese virus" and "kung flu" mirrors the 1800's-era attitude of the "Yellow Peril" and further propagates anti-Asian narratives. Since the pandemic, there have been over 2100 incidents of reported discrimination with over 100 of those qualifying as legal hate crimes.[1] These appalling statistics indicate a greater inability to understand why these abuses continue to take place. As these atrocities committed against Black and brown people continue to amass, the response of American Christianity, with its precepts to love God and neighbor, has been inconsistent at best, and often favors the oppressors.

Nevertheless, there are opportunities for people to learn to be good allies and make change. *Jesus of the East* was written as a counter-narrative to galvanize Christian engagement in the social justice issues, and therefore Christian issues of our time. We as a people, society, and nation are uniquely positioned to confront and improve systems that emphasize and empathize with the wounded in order to heal divisions in our country and world. Being "on the right side of history" can sound like a cliché, but it is also a sobering lens through which to view our legacies. We want to make our descendants proud of our moral courage, and nothing bends towards justice without us bending it. Through dialogue and listening, reflection and activism, we start to move forward in creating the beloved

---

1   ADL Blog. "Reports of Anti-Asian Assaults, Harassment and Hate Crimes Rise as Coronavirus Spreads." *Anti Defamation League*, 18 June 2020, www.adl.org/blog/reports-of-anti-asian-assaults-harassment-and-hate-crimes-rise-as-coronavirus-spreads.

community that many of us are seeking to share.

Preparing for Discussion and How to Use this Guide:

Whether you are a leader or participant within your group, this guide is designed to lead your through group discussion as well as personal reflection:

The guide is structured according to the book's chapters so that your group may focus on particular parts of the text that they found the most interesting and/or difficult. For each chapter, there is a section with discussion questions, suggested practices, and resources that would benefit readers seeking further information. These are resources that Luu turned to in writing *Jesus of the East*.

The content and structure of the guide is intended to be accessible and helpful to a number of audiences. You may be coming to the book as a faithful follower of Western Christianity who is seeking to revise your relationship to the gospels; you may be a person who has been hurt by the strictures of the Western church. Even then, the differentiation between the wounded and those who have caused harm is rarely ever clean-cut. Each group will be different, and even within groups, folks will be coming from different perspectives. Questions are structured so that group members may gradually open up to one another and begin learning together—depending on your group's rapport and knowledge of the book's subjects, you can pick and choose questions to personalize the experience. Furthermore, you will find that a number of questions have different versions depending on your group's needs and demographics. It is up to your group as a team to be aware of this and to choose questions and approaches beforehand in order to appropriately welcome all members into the conversation.

Before you begin reading *Jesus of the East*, consider starting a journal. For each chapter's Practices section, we've included writing prompts that group members can engage with either in private or during shared time. They are intended to both aid group members in examining their own spiritual journeys, and to allow folks who may be less comfortable sharing aloud to process their thoughts and feelings in an impactful manner.

Please consider the following suggestions for approaching discussion:

- Keep the topics relevant by using I-statements rather than generalities. "'I've come to realize" or "I find this confusing" rather than "They always say this." The point of discussion is not debate, but to clarify and help open minds.

- Be respectful of another person's ideas and attitudes. If you want to respond differently, often it is helpful to say, "I've not experienced it this way" or "I would rather think of it like this..."

- Give examples of how you have been affected by an idea and what it might mean for you.

From the Introduction to *Jesus of the East*

> "Today, Christianity must be reappropriated again by reclaiming it from the clutches of theological traditions that have perpetuated the victimization of people, our bodies, the land, and the relationships around us. The Christian faith must be returned to the people to whom it rightfully belongs and for whom it was intended—those who are wounded and who have been sinned against" (13-14).
>
> "I hope that, through these pages, Christians will see Jesus with new eyes and therefore become co-creators of a world that dispels the myths of the past, fully embracing the evangelion, or good news" (20).

Questions:

1. *Jesus of the East* asks readers to use this material as a pathway into entering difficult conversations with respect and humility. Luu is not asking you, the reader, to change your mind per se, but to "consider these ideas as a possible way out of our current dilemma" (19). Whether the ideas presented throughout this book are familiar to you or new and challenging, the process of reading and discussing will encourage self-examination—thinking about where we come from, our own possible biases, biases leveled against us, and the weight of our experiences—in order to explore new ideas and generate calls-to-action. Luu even models this practice in the text as he shares reflections and personal narrative spanning across his forty-year faith journey. Ease into your discussion by getting a sense of where each person is coming from.

- If you are not a practicing Christian, what is your relationship to, or understanding of, Western Christianity and the church? How do you practice your beliefs, even if you are an agnostic or atheist?

- If you are a practicing Christian, where are you currently at in your faith journey? What underpins your faith? What are you presently struggling with?

- For all: Why did you pick up *Jesus of the East*? What are you hoping you get out of your reading and discussion of the book? Where might your individual journey lead you next?

2. Let's start with this quote from the introduction: "The demise of Christianity may come not from an increasingly secular world, but from the type of Christianity that presently exists. Perhaps a better question than whether Christianity will survive in today's age is the question of *which kind* of Christianity and *whose Jesus* will be passed down to our theological descendants" (15).

- When people reject Western Christianity or God, why do you think they are doing so? What about Western Christianity are they rejecting?

- If you are not someone who practices Christianity, why is that? What about the depiction of God, Jesus, or their followers does not appeal to you?

- Using the text as a guiding point, how does the presentation of Jesus in the Western church diverge from the portrayal of Jesus in the Gospels? How are the portrayals consistent?

3. Luu argues in the first sentence that "[t]he history of Christianity is one of cultural appropriation," and that it is time for the religion to be reappropriated for the wounded and sinned against (13).

- Begin by discussing the quotation—what are your reactions to this statement and its implications?
- Identify specific instances of cultural appropriation that you have noticed within the community of the Western church, or by the church in the larger political world.
- How have you been wounded by this appropriation of Christianity?

4. *Concluding activity:* Ultimately, for change to occur within ourselves, our faith communities, and the world at large, we must first envision what a restored world and future looks like. After all, using our imaginations offers hope; the act of envisioning the future is a critical step and guiding light for moving forward. With this in mind, write your thoughts on a shared document, group chat, whiteboard, etc.—make sure to save it so you can reference it later. You will want to add to it as you continue to read!

- In what ways do you think the Western church, generally speaking, can revise and/or correct their practices? You could also consider your church more specifically.
- What does a fully reappropriated Christianity that benefits and aids all—particularly the sinned against, the wounded, and the oppressed—look like to you?
- What other ideas do you want your group to thoughtfully consider as you read and discuss?
- After brainstorming as a group, allow private time to think, journal, or talk in pairs. Pick the questions you find most relevant and appropriate to you:
  - What can you personally invest to initiate the changes your group discussed?
  - If you are a follower of Jesus, what depiction of Jesus do you want to pass on to family, friends, and the next generation?

- If you are not religiously affiliated, or practice another faith, what "version" of Jesus do you want to see existing in the world? What version of Jesus is the one that you would like to know?

Practices:

1. *Journal Prompt, before and after group discussion:*

   a. As we enter into this conversation, which is both personal and political, you will be asked to examine yourself and your actions. Your journal is a wonderful place to include personal thoughts, revelations, and meditations. The privacy of the journal will allow a private space to be honest with and critical of yourself, which is a necessary part of growth. You'll also have documentation of your growth and learning process that you can return to in the future. Use the journal as much as you want beyond the provided prompts to take notes on the chapters or to document your experiences with the other Practices.

   b. After reading the introduction and before meeting as a group, write for 5-10 minutes on the following questions: What do you see as contributing factors to our nation's current state of discord and mass disenfranchisement? What do you feel are contributing factors? Of course, you can write from personal experience if this discord has a harmful impact on your life. You can also spend time considering the impact you've observed it having on other communities. After you have your group discussion and listen to the perspectives of your other group members, return to your journal. Write on the same topic for another 5 to 10 minutes. Consider the ways in which your writing or thoughts have changed.

2. If you regularly pray, begin incorporating new prayers into your routine.

    - Read some of the prayers in the back of the *Book of Common Prayer* nightly, or as a meditative practice in the morning. You can order a copy online or find it at www.bcponline.org

    - Reach out to friends or family who participate in other faith traditions and ask them to share common prayers. Luu's recommendation is to start with *Peace is Every Step* by Thích Nhất Hạnh!

    - Once you've done more reading, consider commonalities and differences across faith communities in the way that prayer is practiced or written. What are some differences that you were introduced to that you would like to adopt into your own routine?

3. Write your own prayer for the sinned against. If you do not pray, you can try other forms of empathic writing, such as letters, poems, songs, or even visual art.

    - If you are writing a prayer for your own community that has been sinned against, consider sharing it with loved ones as an act of healing.

    - If you are writing a prayer for another community, be sure to avoid passive or even condescending language. Think about your own possible accountability in their hurt as you write. Part of your prayer could be a personal commitment to action—speak to God about concrete steps you might take to be a good ally.

    - Memorize your prayer. Print it off and put it on your fridge. Add it to your daily prayer practice.

Resources:

1.   Claiborne, Shane and Jonathan Wilson-Hartgrove. *Common Prayer: A Liturgy for Ordinary Radicals.* Nashville, TN: Zondervan, 2012.

2.   Hạnh, Thích Nhất. *Peace is Every Step.* New York: Bantam, 1992.

3.   Kruse, Kevin. *One Nation Under God: How Corporate America Invented Christian America.* Princeton University: Basic Books, 2015.

4.   *The Book of Common Prayer.* New York: Church Publishing, 1979.
     a.   Can be found online at www.bcponline.org

5.   Lonergan, Bernard J.F. *Philosophical and Theological Papers, 1958-1964.* Edited by Robert C. Croken, vol. 6, University of Toronto Press, 1996.

Chapter 1: Vision

> "By using insider language to separate 'us' and 'them,' we are attempting to anesthetize ourselves to the painful reality that the world in which are living is not ours. We do not own this land. We do not own this world. Notions of dominion are fictions of the mind. The painful reality is that we are all called to live as foreigners" (29).

> "The great gift of life is to exist as a participant in a life and world that is not entirely our own. It is a constant invitation to love what is not our own, and thereby receive the possibility and joy of love returned. We are part of an intricate tapestry of relationships: with others, with the earth, with animals, with the air. We can no more claim ownership of any of it than we can claim ownership of the sun and stars" (29).

> "Jesus' mission was to liberate people who were caught in oppressive systems and to bring healing to those hurt by them" (31).

Questions:

1. Chapter 1, "Vision," is largely focused on sharing the historical narrative of Jesus of the Gospels, and outlining the kind of people he calls his followers to be. With previous questions, you began to scrutinize your own faith journey and beliefs—now is the time to contemplate your life at large. Depending on the size of your group, you may want to break into smaller groups or pairs.

    a. What is your story? This might be a good time to ask group members to work on a six-word memoir. For example, Luu's is: Child of war, piecing together life.

    b. How has your personal history influenced the life you

lead today?

   c.   Why do you think *Jesus of the East* will be important for you? Do you think it will challenge you? If yes, how so?

2.   Refresh yourself on the section that begins under the subject heading "Between Two Worlds" (26) and ends on page 28 with the sentence "Jesus and his followers lived in the same way, as foreigners." Perhaps you find yourself coming to the book as an "inbetweener," or part of a marginalized group, such as Luu, or perhaps you are unfamiliar with this experience. Those who have been sinned against should be given the opportunity to speak first.

- If you are an "inbetweener," part of a marginalized group, or have been sinned against, how has your experience affected the way you move through the world? How has it affected your ability to connect to the church and the way Christianity is practiced in the West?

- If you are unfamiliar with the experience of being an "inbetweener," consider Luu's experience, or the experience of a friend who has trusted you with their story.

  - Can you envision a way in which living as an "inbetweener" may affect one's connection to a church, country, or society that has turned its back on the people forced into the margins? What have you learned from reading Luu's story?

  - Going forward, spend time listening to what other members of the group have to say, and turn to the Resources section of this guide to read more about the experience of marginalized folks, explained in their own words. It is crucial to be a good listener and to not project your own opinions onto your neighbor's experiences.

3. This chapter asks the reader to rethink notions of citizenship. Citizenship has been a contested issue in America for centuries as the term invokes questions of American patriotism, white colonization of native land, and immigration laws. Luu argues that Christians should consider themselves citizens of the larger, geographically undefined kingdom of God. As a result, "Christians might be called to do many culturally and legally unacceptable things and may even go to prison for the kingdom of God. Kingdom citizens should easily abandon national citizenship when the requirements of their nation are in opposition to their commitments as citizens in God's kingdom" (32).

    •   To understand the text, we must understand how citizenship is conceptualized in America and the church. What are you a citizen of? How do you prioritize your various citizenships—which are more important to you? What groups or identities form your self-conception, or affect the way that others perceive you?

    •   In what ways is an idea of citizenship with boundaries—geographic, financial, etc.—harmful to people and/or to the vision of God's kingdom?

    •   What do you think of Luu's call to abandon national citizenship in favor of citizenship to the kingdom? How does this make you? Hopeful? Uncomfortable? Why?

4. Refresh yourself on the two paragraphs under the heading "Western Visions of Jesus and the Kingdom," which beings on page 38. These paragraphs discuss Minjung, *han*, and liberation theology.

    •   You can start by discussing your immediate reactions to this vision of a theology for the people, or Minjung.

Discuss what might this concept mean for you?

- If you are part of any faith group or church, in what ways does your group already practice facets of Minjung theology, i.e. focusing on healing of the oppressed or wounded? What could this theology and way of thinking offer your group?

- If you do not follow Jesus, in what ways does this theology change your understanding of Jesus and his message? How might it conflict with your current understanding of Western Christianity? What does this theology or way of living have to offer the world at large?

5. *Concluding Activity:* As you did after reading the introduction, and as the chapter title encourages, spend time envisioning or reimagining a future for Christianity, guided by the principles of Minjung theology and citizenship of God's Kingdom. If you follow Jesus, envisioning a new kingdom of God requires us to strip ourselves bare of things that make us comfortable and to leave behind the ways in which we've constructed our lives that might hurt others and prevent healing.

- What are comfort and/or blind spots that you have that are preventing you from working towards a vision of God's kingdom without boundaries?

- What would it look like to "birth another way of living" in your own life regardless of your religious affiliations (30)? If you are a Christian, what are your first steps to take up Luu's call to reconsider your citizenship?

Practices:

1. *Journal Prompt, after group discussion:* In this chapter, Luu asks what it might look like if we pursue stillness, and to allow

ourselves to become emotionally and spiritually stripped bare, as Jesus was in the desert. As he points out, "[t]he desert to which God calls us may not be a physical place. But can be found in any space that allows us to be stripped of the things that enslave us and make us less human" (36). Try writing on the following questions in order to explore the idea of your own liberation and your own metaphorical desert.

- What is weighing you down? What burdens and expectations are placed on you by society? What burdens and expectations might you be placing on yourself?

- Imagine the best possible life for yourself. What would emotional, spiritual, or even physical liberation look like?

- What could you do to give yourself space to enter your own metaphorical desert? How can you make yourself more vulnerable in order to fully explore and see the nature of your existence? If you are able to take the actions you brainstormed, do so, and come back to journal about the results.

- Please remember, these ideas may feel destabilizing for you. Doubt, fear, exhaustion, hesitation—these feelings are natural and even useful in emotional metamorphoses. Use your journal to lay out your most difficult feelings and to be fully honest without yourself.

2. Gather a group of friends together and hold a screening of Kevin Miller's documentary *J.E.S.U.S.A.*, an in-depth exploration of the relationship between Christianity and American nationalism. Hold space for an honest and vulnerable post-screening discussion of the film and its relevance to viewers' spiritual journeys, especially in regard to US nationalism. In the Resources section, you'll find many suggested films that you could also

watch as a group or on your own.

3. It is time to *show up* and *lean in* for marginalized communities, meaning to actively listen and participate in issues of social justice. In the language of *Jesus of the East,* we are asked "to listen and be changed" just like Jesus (26). There are many online activities to participate in that encourage dialogue, education, and transformation, particularly in the aftermath of police brutality against people of color and the LGBTQIA+ community. These conversations require respect and a structured approach, but experienced leaders—particularly BIPOC and LGBTQIA+ leaders, or leaders representing diverse voices—are adept at facilitating these outside of the church or your faith. With an open heart, reach out, listen, and learn. Seek out structured conversations about allyship, race, immigration, or another issue that you don't know much about. These are starting points for engaging in concrete action—you can then carry your learnings back to your faith community and your own practice. This step might take you some Googling and asking around, but here's a good place to start: The Metro DC Synod is hosting a four-part online workshop series called "Imago Dei" as a part of their Racial Equity Initiative (www.metrodcelca.org/imagodei/).

4. Another way to show up by educating yourself is to rethink your social media feeds. What you see every day—the posts, the comments, the videos—affects how you think, and how you see the world. Follow diverse groups and individuals that are engaged in fights for justice and equity. Consider that the process of healing and justice for oppressed groups is an intersectional issue—even if you are part of a marginalized group, what intersection of healing are you not as familiar with? Show up and improve your practice. "Listen and be changed."

5.   As you begin doing more research and referring to the Resources provided in this discussion guide, you'll find a number of worthy causes for racial justice and equality, among many other social issues. If you are able to donate, please do so. Some folks within the Christian community have even chosen to calculate their tithes and put that money partially or entirely towards organizations such as the ACLU and the NAACP, for example. If you are not able to donate at this time, you can always share donation information on social media, and bookmark causes to donate to when/if you are able.

Resources:

1.   The following films, miniseries, and documentaries are all available on streaming services and are excellent tools for sparking dialogue:

   a.   *J.E.S.U.S.A.* (Miller, 2020)

      i.   Rent through the creators' website at http://watch.jesusafilm.com/

   b.   *True Justice: Bryan Stevenson's Fight for Equality* (Kunhardt, 2019)

   c.   *Just Mercy* (Cretton, 2019)

   d.   *13th* (DuVernay, 2016)

   e.   *When They See Us* (DeVernay, 2019)

   f.   *Immigration Nation* (Clusiau and Schwarz, 2020)

   g.   *Disclosure: Trans Lives on Screen* (Feder, 2020)

2.   The Equal Justice Initiative, founded by Bryan Stevenson (author of *Just Mercy*), has many ideas for how to participate in the efforts for criminal justice reform and racial equity.

   a.   Find these materials at https://eji.org/ and consider donating through the "Donate" button at the bottom of the page.

3. Metro DC Synod of the Evangelical Lutheran Church's Racial Equity Initiative has reading lists, educational series, and a downloadable *White Privilege Toolkit* online.
    a. Find these materials at http://metrodcelca.org/racial-equity/

4. Nguyen, Viet Thanh. *Nothing Ever Dies: Vietnam and the Memory of War*. Cambridge, MA: Harvard University Press, 2011.

5. Martin, Michel. "Slave Bible from the 1800s Omitted Key Passages That Could Incite Rebellion." *All Things Considered*, December 9, 2018. https://www.npr.org/2018/12/ 09/674995075/ slave-bible-from-the-1800s-omitted-key-passages-that-could-incite-rebellion.

6. MacIntyre, Alasdair. *Whose Justice? Which Rationality*? Notre Dame, IN: University of Notre Dame Press, 1988.

7. Shermer, Michael. "The Number of Americans with No Religious Affiliation Is Rising." *Scientific American*, Springer Nature America, Inc., 1 Apr. 2018.

8. Dick, Phillip K. *The Man in the High Castle*. New York: G. P. Putnam's Sons, 1962.

9. Irenaeus. *Against Heresies*. In *The Apostolic Fathers with Justin Martyr and Irenaeus*, edited by Philip Schaff. Grand Rapids, MI: Eerdmans, 2001. Originally published as *Libros quinque adversus haereses*. Edited by W. Wigan Harvey. Cambridge, UK: Typis.

10. Augustine, Sermon 117. For the English, see *Sermon on the Mount; Harmony of the Gospels; Homilies on the Gospels*, trans. R. G. MacMullen, vol. 6 of *Nicene and Post-Nicene Fathers*, Series 1, ed. Philip Schaff (Grand Rapids, MI: Eerdmans), 963.

11. Origen of Alexandria. *Origen: Contra Celsum*. Translated by Henry Chadwick. Cambridge, UK: Cambridge University Press, 1980.

Chapter 2:
Birth, Beginnings, and the Body

66 "It is through this tender flesh that we relate to one another. We know each other in our bodies before we have fully gained conscious awareness of who we are. In these bodies, we reach out to our mothers to grasp and suckle. In these bodies, we express our deepest yearnings through noises and sounds. In these bodies, some form value systems that privilege some bodies over others" (56).

"Jesus' story is our own story. Just as we live our lives in the flesh and in our own particular bodies, so Jesus lived his life in the flesh of his particular body" (60).

"God's involvement in human history was not solely to solve a problem, but it was and is a story of abandonment and love that is grounded in relationships with people and with the world in which we live" (64).
99

Questions:

1. "The problem of race is the problem of how we view and treat the body," Luu writes (55). Think about your own life experiences. In what ways have you personally experienced or witnessed value systems where some bodies are privileged over others? See pp. 55-56 for a list with a few examples. If you enter this discussion having researched and educated yourself on current political issues so that you have an awareness of what is occurring both nationally and locally, your discussion will be infinitely richer.

- Throughout the chapter, it becomes apparent that Cartesian modes of dualistic thought have informed Western Christianity. Dualism, in short, proposes a separation of the mind and body, and interpretations of it often encourage us to prize thoughts over concrete experience and action.

  - Using the discussion of dualism on pages 62 and 63, spend time considering how this type of thinking and theology minimizes human experience. As an exercise, examine specific language such as "I'm colorblind" or "all lives matter"—examine their philosophical roots and, thus, their context in issues of social justice and racism. In what ways is this kind of language particularly harmful and diminishing to marginalized populations?

  - Reflect on your personal experience. How have you personally been hurt by rhetoric that diminishes your bodily experiences? Share your personal experience if you feel comfortable doing so. Together or individually, you may need space to express frustration and hurt. If you prefer to not share aloud, you could take a private moment to journal.

  - Discuss ways in which dualistic thinking and rhetoric that denies lived experiences are present both in the church and the larger political landscape. How do these two spaces—the political and the religious—inform one another? If you *showed up* and participated in the Practices for the first few chapters, you may have watched *J.E.S.U.S.A*, and can apply what you learned to this conversation.

2. Luu argues that it is essential for our reading of the Jesus of the Gospels to be connected with issues of justice—Jesus' life *was* not

and *is* not separate from social and ecological matters. Instead, such concerns should be fully reintegrated into our practice of Christianity. Why is the incarnation of God significant for giving context to modern social issues and lived experiences, such as how we treat and police POC and LGBTQIA+ folks?

3. *Closing activity:* As we seek to stand with and love our neighbors who have been othered by the church and our society, we must understand that we can never fully know the life of another, just as Jesus could not fully know the physical experience of being a woman or an Asian-American man despite experiencing his own forms of persecution. The questions that Luu poses at the end of the chapter (78) provide us with starting points to reflect and actively practice better fellowship. Using a shared document or mind map, brainstorm how you might follow in the footsteps of Jesus of the Gospels.

   - If you are coming to the book as one who has been sinned against or oppressed:
     - What expectations do you have for your neighbors and those who have hurt you? When have you been failed and how does that make you feel?
     - Hold space for healing as a group. Verbally validate one another's experiences. This may be as simple as saying, "I believe you" or "I am here next to you," or other gestures and expressions that work to uplift another person as they're speaking.
     - Unifying the voices of those who are different yet also hurting can be a powerful tool for forming community and affecting change. Thus, in what ways might you also risk being *enfleshed*, and standing beside those who are different from you yet also hurting?

- If you are religious, consider ending with a group prayer without a clear leader. Let people speak as they want—in full sentences or even single words—to ask for prayers or healing, and to express rage or joy.

- If you are not part of a marginalized group, or are coming to the book with a recognition of your own privilege or even complicity:

  - What are ways that you can risk being *enfleshed* beings and walk with others?

  - How can you leave your places of comfort to form vulnerable relationships with those whose lives are outside your spheres of comfort and safety, in order to enter into community?

  - How might you adjust your worldviews to come to know God's body as the body of the oppressed and the marginalized, the body of those who are unjustly put down in the world?

  - Whether or not you are religious or faithful, ask yourself how you may positively take part in the healing of the *han*-afflicted without demanding center stage or pressing your own beliefs.

Practices:

1. *Journal Prompt, after discussion:* In discussing issues of marginalization, and in learning how to *show up* and *lean in* for the sake of healing, we must continue to perform difficult self-evaluation and hold ourselves accountable. Spend time to be honest with yourself.

   - In what ways have you see yourself fall short recently when it comes to racial justice or other forms of justice?

     - What has been your experience with those who profess to being *colorblind* or asserted that *all lives matter*? How have people used similar language with a different issue? Examine the motivations behind your actions if this has been your language. Particularly if you say these things with good intentions—does the impact of your statements line up with your intentions?

- Consider your behavior beyond social media or in your own family. How do you carry yourself in your classroom, workspace, or place of worship? How do you hold yourself accountable in all spaces—public and private?

- How have your opinions or relationship to language and justice changed after reading this chapter?

2. Particularly if you live in a predominantly white or wealthy neighborhood, make a point to acquaint yourself with the housing politics of your city.

- Pay attention to where boundaries have been established (either by actual city/zone lines, and/or by predominant demographics). You can likely find coverage of these issues in your local newspaper.

- Seek ways to support low income and BIPOC communities in your city. For example, begin shopping at local BIPOC business rather than large corporate chains.

- Look especially at who is a part of your own faith community and who is most obviously welcome. Ask questions about how church leaders are actively working to encourage diversity in your community. Even if your congregation is visually diverse, are there platforms for diversity of thought and voices—are BIPOC & LGBTQIA+ folks given equal voice? How can you be of service to this cause?

3. Swap out a trip you were planning to take for pleasure for a trip to the Edmund Pettis Bridge in Selma, Alabama. Organize a group of friends or your family to go to the Equal Justice Initiative's Legacy Museum in Montgomery, Alabama, the National Museum of African American History and Culture in DC, or the National Museum of the American Indian also in DC, to suggest a few. If you can't make it to these spots physically, many offer virtual tours.

Resources:

1. Viet Thanh Nguyen's project, *Another War Memorial*, is an online memorial for the American War in Vietnam "featuring oral histories of the war's witnesses and testimonies to the dead." In this project, Nguyen and his students question why certain memorials honor U.S. soldiers who participated in the war, but not others who died, such as Vietnamese citizens.

    a. Learn more at www.anotherwarmemorial.com

2. Emerson, Michael and Christian Smith. *Divided by Faith: Evangelical Religion and the problem of Race in America.* New York: Oxford University Press, 2001.

3. Duncan, Lenny. *Dear Church: A Love Letter from a Black Preacher to the Whitest Denomination in the US.* Minneapolis, MN: Fortress Press, 2019.

4. Check out Fr. Daniel G. Groody's entire body of work on the theology of migration. Specifically, *Globalization, Spirituality and Justice: Navigating the Path to Peace.* Maryknoll, NY: Orbis Books, 2007.

5. Duck, Ruth C. "Hospitality to Victims: A Challenge for Christian Worship." In *The Other Side of Sin: Woundedness from the Perspective of the Sinned-Against*, edited by Andrew Sung Park

and Susan L. Nelson, 165–180. Albany: State University of New York Press, 2001.re

6. U.S. Census Bureau. "About Race." U.S. Census, last revised January 23, 2018. https:// www.census.gov/topics/population/race/about.html.

7. Somashekhar, Sandhya. "The Disturbing Reason Some African American Patients May Be Undertreated for Pain." *Washington Post*, April 4, 2016. https://www.washington post.com/news/to-your-health/wp/2016/04/04/doblacks-feel-less-pain-than-whites-their-doctors-may-think-so/.

8. Lee, Jasmine C., and Haeyoun Park. "15 Black Lives Ended in Confrontations with Police. 3 Officers Convicted." *New York Times*, updated October 5, 2018, https:// www.nytimes.com/interactive/2017/05/17/us/black-deaths-police.html.

9. Wallis, Jim. *America's Original Sin: Racism, White Privilege, and the Bridge to a New America*. Grand Rapids, MI: Brazos Press, 2017.

10. Williams, Reggie L. *Bonhoeffer's Black Jesus: Harlem Renaissance Theology and an Ethic of Resistance*. Waco, TX: Baylor University Press, 2014.

11. Ross, Ellen M. *The Grief of God: Images of the Suffering God in Late Medieval England*. Oxford: Oxford University Press, 1997.

12. Hannam, James. *The Genesis of Science: How the Christian Middle Ages Launched the Scientific Revolution*. Washington, DC: Regnery Publishing, 2011.

13. Gregory of Nazianzus. "Ep. 101 (To Cledonius)." In *Cyril of Jerusalem, Gregory Nazianzen*. Vol. 7 of *The Nicene and Post-Nicene Fathers*, Series 2, edited by Philip Schaff. Grand Rapids, MI: Eerdmans, 2007.

14. Ignatius. *The Epistle of Ignatius to the Smyrnaeans*. Page 297 in *Clement. II Clement. Ignatius. Polycarp. Didache*. Vol. 1 of *The Apostolic Fathers*, edited and translated by Bart D. Ehrman.

Cambridge, MA: Harvard University Press, 2003.

Chapter 3: Sinners, Sin, *Han*, and the Mission of Jesus

66 "Jesus proclaimed a liberation that was not restricted by nation or tribe to his own people" (87).

"Jesus' mission was not to rescue people from the fires of hell and eternal punishment—no one who has become lost wants to be lost or deserves to be labeled a 'sinner' as a result. Rather, those who are lost are like sheep who have wandered from the fold and need protection from the perils of predators" (89).

"The healing of *han* is challenging because there is no quick or easy fix. Simply saying that Jesus will heal the *han* of the world will not accomplish that healing. . . In speaking of a healing community, I am speaking of something larger than the church or any particular denominations. . . in order for the deep divides in our culture to be resolved, we cannot remain in separate groups and ideologies. We need thoughtful programs of reconciliation and healing that move us beyond diversity training and cultural awareness" (106-07). 99

Questions:

1. As we delve deeper into the study of sin and the mission of Jesus, begin your discussions with a welcoming platform and relatively open-ended questions. What passages in this chapter struck you, made you uncomfortable, or even made you rethink your own actions? Allow time for 3 to 5 people to answer, or form smaller groups for discussion. Don't feel pressured to turn each answer

into a full conversation—unless someone makes a harmful comment that needs to be addressed, simply encourage folks to make "I" statements about the text.

2. The subtitle of *Jesus of the East*, "Reclaiming the Gospel for the Wounded," evokes a doctrine of Christianity where the emphasis moves from the sinner and the sinner's forgiveness to the healing of sinned against.

   - What does Christianity look like if we shift the lens to those who have been and are being sinned against?
   - In what ways would your personal practice as a Christian change? What privilege would you need to give up?

3. *Han* is a nearly untranslatable Korean word which means something close to *the deep wounded suffering of people*. This book is not only about Jesus, but it is about—quite simply— healing *han*. Discuss your initial reactions to the term *han*.

   - In English, we have few, if any, words that can capture the complexity of the meaning of *han*. What situations have you seen or experienced in the world that could be describe as an experience of *han*?
   - What is the danger of not recognizing and taking steps to treat the trauma associated with the *han* of the sinned against?
   - Discuss ways in which *Jesus of the East* suggests that *han* can be healed.
   - According to the text, whose job is it to do the healing of *han* within the world? Where do you personally fall on the spectrum of this call to action?

4. Today's world is often divided into false binaries and labels that contribute to structures of oppression, such as Black/white, gay/

straight, and man/woman, to name a few. Jesus' ancient world was not immune to these harmful, deceptively simple binaries. In fact, as alluded to throughout the chapter, the church's religious leaders were responsible for establishing these troubling dichotomies. The church created a dichotomy in which "[t]he 'sinners' are those who do not believe in and conform to certain moral codes, while the holy people are those in the church" (100).

- How has a church adhering to these false dualities harmed those who have historically been considered outside the flock?
- What must be done to move away from these dichotomies of who is and isn't "in communion" (101)?
- How have our religious ideas of the past contributed to the church and ourselves committing the sin of excluding or actively hurting whole groups of people or individuals?

5. Luu redefines sin as "a violation of the law of love towards God, humans, and the Earth" (102). In redefining sin, Luu attempts to illuminate the root of many problems in our modern world, allowing us to treat the sickness and not just the symptoms.

- Discuss this definition. How is it useful or not useful?
- Depending on your answer to the question above, your group can spend time creating their own definition of sin that reimagines it not as an inherent evil of humanity, but as an action or thought that creates disharmony. How might your definition seek to address the "sickness" and not just the "symptoms"?

6. *Concluding activity, option 1:* "Jesus proclaimed a liberation that was not restricted by nation or tribe to his own people, and he offered examples of non-Jewish foreigners who would receive

the blessings of freedom and healing" (87). As with the previous chapters, spend time reimagining your Christian faith. Envision a future in which Jesus is not simply a historical figure whose actions and teachings are selectively disseminated and practiced by the Western Church, but a manifestation of God who is deeply connected to modern global liberation.

- What would you want a Christianity concerned with justice to look like? Consider ways that you may variegate your approach by seeking voices, educational opportunities, and healing communities outside of the church or religion. What institutions can you look to outside of the church to find healing communities and solutions for justice?

- Search for churches that provide an aspirational model, either through Googling or by asking friends who attend other churches, and study what they do.

7. *Concluding activity, option 2:* The terms "other" and "othering," outside of quotidian usage, are significant philosophical and sociological concepts. A simple definition from dictionary.com defines *othering* as: "to view or treat someone or a group of people as intrinsically different and alien for oneself." As Luu explains in this chapter, the othering of certain groups of people have led to marginalization, oppression, and the accumulation of *han* for those communities. With the following questions, take a look at your own community, be it your city, or smaller communities: your household, faith group, workplace, etc. And again, healing and oppression are intersectional issues. Even as you may be a victim of *han*, you may participate in the oppression of other groups. Pick question(s) below according to what you think is most appropriate for your group:

- Who is "in" and who is clearly othered in your

community? Faith leaders—allow an open space for criticism and validation for those who have been hurt and directly witnessed hurt.

- If you are personally a victim of othering, oppression, or *han*, what rules or behaviors have been harmful to your community? What rules or behaviors even within your community have been harmful?

- Journal privately for 5-10 minutes. Are there ways in which you have personally estranged a particular group of people? What steps can you take to allow for greater access? Start with the smallest community you can think of—your own home, your reading group, or your faith community. Share a few of your ideas as a way to close out your meeting.

- Note: Group leaders, do you research ahead of time! Bring reputable articles or materials that reference specific events and laws to facilitate a constructive and factual conversation.

Practices:

1. *Journal Practice*: While *Jesus of the East* issues a call to action to those who have actively inflicted *han*, Luu also seeks to share a liberative gospel that directly benefits the wounded and the sinned against. Chapter 3 works to deconstruct harmful notions such as the inherency of sin. In recounting an experience with a Catholic sister, he draws attention to the sin of the church as it constructs ideas of who is "in" and "out of communion" with God (101).

   - Once again, be vulnerable with yourself. How has the Western church's actions and rhetoric damaged you? Has the church sinned against you by treating you as inherently sinful, rejecting you, or othering you? Has the church inflicted you with *han*, whether or not you are a practicing Christian? If you prefer, you can consider society at large.

- Consider the way you treat yourself as a result. Can you differentiate between holding yourself accountable for sinful acts—committing "a violation of the law of love towards God, humans and the Earth"—versus the sinful language of the church or society that seeks to make you feel guilty as an oppressive measure?

- Reader, as you explore your own history and emotions, you may find that you punish yourself because you have been taught that you are sinful due to your sexuality, gender identity, race, income, or other factors. How does this make you feel? What would it look like if you worked towards self-healing and towards forgiving yourself?

2. Engage in an act of "curative sorrow" through seeking or making art (73). For Christian communities, this might mean including images of a wounded Christ in your private worship area, or listening to hymns of justice and sorrow alone or as a group. If you are not a follower of Jesus, you might research art focused more generally on activism and justice, and share with your group. For example, check out this luminous hymn entitled "It Is Enough" by Pastor R. DeAndre Johnson, a friend of Luu's, on YouTube: https://youtu.be/DqSyIIXHmzQ Generally speaking, if you find an artist you like, consider purchasing something from them! Now is the time to support BIPOC, queer, and working-class artists who are speaking truth to power. Alternatively, you can support them through your local public museum's gallery showings.

3. Remain engaged. In order to avoid repeating the sins of the past,

we need to stay vigilant as to how our actions today might reflect those prior sins. Read widely. Listen to trusted podcasts. There are several ways to engage in conversations led by theologians, historians, and educators, who are persistently involved in this kind of kingdom work. Take time to load your smart device with some of these resources, or subscribe to newsletters, or periodicals that will keep you aware and encouraged in an ongoing practice of doing this work. The list underneath this chapter's Resources section is a fantastic starting point.

Resources:
1. Podcasts, magazines, and newsletters are great starting points for breaking open the most difficult political conversations. There are many good resources available, often for free. Luu suggests checking out the magazines *The Christian Century, Sojourners,* and *Christianity Today.* Podcasts are especially amazing, since you can listen throughout your day as you're driving or doing chores. Here are some good starting points:
   - *Mere Fidelity* with Malcolm Foley—Foley is a Ph.D. candidate at Baylor University doing work on race for the church. A good episode to begin with is entitled "Lynchings, Protests, and Unrest: Racism in America"
   - *(Re)thinking Faith* with Eugene Cho—Cho is the author of *Thou Shalt Not Be a Jerk: A Christian's Guide to Engaging Politics.* He speaks about how a Christian, or anyone for that matter, can talk about politics without being a jerk.
   - *Talking Theology*—Voices from across the pond with Bishop Guli Francis-Dehqani, an Iranian-British priest presiding over Loughborough, in the Diocese of Leicester (Canterbury). She is working with African, Asian, and other minority communities in her parish.

Check out the episode entitled, "How is a theology of racial diversity part of the Good News today?"

2. Park, Andrew Sung. *The Triune Atonement: Christ's Healing for Sinners, Victims, and the Whole of Creation*. Louisville, KY: Westminster John Knox, 2014.

3. ———."The Bible and *Han*." In *The Other Side of Sin: Woundedness from the Perspective of the Sinned-Against*, edited by Andrew Sung Park and Susan L. Nelson, 45–59. Albany: State University of New York Press, 2001.

4. ———. *Racial Conflict and Healing: An Asian American Theological Perspective*. Eugene, OR: Wipf and Stock, 2009.

5. Federal Bureau of Investigations. "2017 Hate Crime Statistics: Incidents and Offenses." FBI, accessed January 4, 2020, https://ucr.fbi.gov/hate-crime/2017/topic-pages/incidents-and-offenses.

6. "Read Obama's Full Speech from the University of Illinois," NBC Chicago, September 8, 2018, https://www.nbcchicago.com/blogs/ward-room/obama-university-of-illinois-full-speech-492719531.html.

7. Emerson, Michael. *Market Cities, People Cities: The Shape of Our Urban Future*. New York: NYU Press, 2018.

8. Nietzsche, Friedrich. On *the Genealogy of Morals*. Translated by Walter Kaufmann and R. J. Hollingdale. New York: Vintage Press, 1989.

9. Weaver, J. Denny. *The Nonviolent Atonement*. Rev. 2nd ed. Grand Rapids, MI: Eerdmans, 2011.

10. Aulén, Gustaf. Christus Victor: *An Historical Study of the Three Main Types of the Idea of Atonement*. Translated by A. G. Hebert. New York: Macmillan, 1969. First published 1931.

11. Hammesfahr, Petra. *The Sinner*. Translated by John Brownjohn, Penguin Books, 2017. Originally published in 1999.

12. Augustine. *Confessions*. Translated by Henry Chadwick. Oxford,

UK: Oxford University Press, 1998.

Chapter 4: God Against the Machine

❝ "Being created in the image of God is not solely a spiritual concept. The image of God is the complete person, body and soul, the entire human, and not only a person's mind" (120).

"Sitting at the table with all people often means we will sit with those we do not like or care to know. We will sit at the table with perceived enemies or those foreign to us. We may be invited to dine with someone of a different ethnicity, cultural background, skin color, political affiliation, sexual orientation, or belief system. Living in the kingdom is a scary prospect, especially for those who have lived under the system of the Pharaoh. To eat with eat other reveals our deepest vulnerabilities: that we share the same hunger and thirst, that we are not exempt from needing others" (125). ❞

Questions:

By now, you have a sense of your group's dynamics. If slow and open-ended warm-up questions work for you, then start with by simply asking for reactions to theories of scarcity and a gospel of abundance. If not, then you can always use the specific prompts listed under question 1, or skip ahead to future questions to personalize your group's experience.

1. Allow an open platform for folks to share their initial reactions to the chapter's discussion of theories of scarcity and a gospel of abundance.
    - Thus far, do you feel that you've been operating under a theory of scarcity, abundance, or something else in your personal life? How does the promise of abundance incite joy, discomfort, or neutrality for you?

- If you find that you default to scarcity or a similar principle, consider delving deeper by asking yourself *why*. Why do you default to scarcity—what is the root of this thinking in your life?

- How has your thoughts about scarcity versus abundance changed after reading the chapter?

- What questions do you have about the different theories offered that you want to tackle as a group? Together, you can dig into the most challenging parts of the chapter.

2. Group leaders can segue from the previous question to a discussion of the paragraph beginning on page 122 with, "The irony of life in the United States is that we are in a land with plentiful resources. . ." Discuss the ways in which the chapter draws a connection between notions of scarcity, and oppressive and damaging institutions such as colonization and white supremacy. As usual, the goal is to not point fingers at other group members, but to gently untangle complicated histories and their impacts which have been woven into our personal belief systems.

- What does it mean to act out of a perspective of scarcity?

- Why is a theory of abundance critical and relevant not simply from a theological standpoint, but when we consider lived human experience?

- Luu shows examples of how the Western church and theories of scarcity can lead to creating injustice and accumulating *han*. What is your perspective on his argument? Does the gospel of abundance feel like the start of a solution to this issue—why or why not?

3. You may be reading this book because you have been wounded, or because you feel outside of, or even rejected by, the Western Christian church. If this is the case, how does it feel to see

discussions of social justice appearing in theology? How does it make you feel to read a book about social justice backed by a study of the life and actions of Jesus?

4. Reread this selection from page 117: "Neither Jesus nor his followers were ever apolitical or nonpolitical. Until Constantine, they were understood to be revolutionaries, offering an alternative to the politics of Rome. The ministry of Jesus continually opposed both a system of scarcity *and* a view of personhood that defined some individuals as 'less than divine' image bearers—a view resulting from a perspective of scarcity. Both of these aspects of Jesus' ministry are political in nature."

    - If your group consists of the wounded and the *han-*inflicted, this can be a time for personal testimony:
        - How have you experienced a system of scarcity as it informs and shapes institutionalized oppression?
        - What is the connection between scarcity and injustice? How is this a useful tool for understanding and dismantling systemized oppression? For seeking liberation? How would you revise or expand upon Luu's analysis?

    - If your group is seeking to be allies to those who are *han-*inflicted, or if the group consists of those who have benefitted from the oppression of others directly or indirectly, this is an opportunity to be self-critical:
        - How have you seen the system of scarcity inform and shape institutionalized racism through economic policies, the criminal justice system, and even the public school system? What other forms of oppression you have seen scarcity inform?
        - How have you seen the Western church actively

dehumanize or ordain certain individuals to be 'less than divine'"? What does this look like in the church? In society as a whole?

- If you are part of a faith group or church, consider your community specifically. How have you seen your own church act out of a perspective of scarcity? How does this impact the church's ministry and community?

- What have you done thus far to intervene or speak out against a system of scarcity? What else needs to be done?

- Without a doubt, this question will be the start of difficult conversations, and may open up wounds. Once you feel like you have made ground as a group, take a break and allow time for personal journaling. Based on what came up in your conversation, ask yourselves: What does a political or revolutionary ministry like that of Jesus look like to you?

5. *Concluding activity:* Join together again after journaling. Diana Butler Bass uses a table as a metaphor for God's kingdom and His abundance. Luu points out that we are asked by God to dine with those who may be "foreign to us" (125). Take a moment to consider who is at your metaphorical table. Who do you regularly "dine" or commune with? As Luu asks on page 127, "What is the divide that must be bridged in order to welcome the stranger into our own homes, places of business, and spheres of influence?"

- For those who have been sinned against, this may be an opportunity to be thankful for your community, or for those from whom you draw strength.

- What tables are you not welcomed at, and how does that make you feel? How do you build community in spite of this?

- What does your table look like? Who are your elders; who offers you guidance?
- Who else should be welcomed to your table that you have not yet engaged with? (E.g. if you are a cisgender man, do you uplift the voices of women in your community? If you're a cisgender woman, do you uplift the voices of transgender folks in your community?)
- What do you want your table to look like as you continue to grow and change? What do you personally want to bring to your table, and pass to younger generations?

- For those who have existed in their safe spaces of the Western Church, intentionally or unintentionally excluding those who are othered by the church, this is an opportunity to be self-critical. Identify your own blind spots.
  - What does your table look like? Mostly white people? Straight or cisgender people? Wealthy people? Only people who look and think like you?
  - You can even consider the group you are reading this book with. What is the demographic of your reading group? Is it intentional or unintentional? Do you have one "token" person who is not demographically homogenous? How has the group depended on this person? Are they often looked upon to explain systems of injustice, or to share their own experiences of *han* so that the majority may understand better?
  - After reflecting on the chapter, spend time considering how you should show up at a table, invited by God,

with those who may be foreign to you.

Practices:

1. *Journal Prompt, after group discussion:* Continue to meditate on Butler's idea of the table—allow yourself space to think for a few days before engaging with this journal prompt, if that feels right to you. For this prompt, let's take the idea of the table from the conceptual realm to a more practical one. From page 125-127, Luu discusses the practice of hospitality—what does and should hospitality look like in your daily life? How might you seek the restoration that Luu discusses at the end of the chapter (139)?

   - If you have been sinned against, what expectations do you have for those who have perpetuated your hurt? What sort of internal work must your community do for healing? Of course, all communities are multivocal— even within your community, you may not be fully supported or you might not fully support others. What sort of internal work must your community do to be as hospitable and abundant as possible for all members?

   - If you are a person with privilege, a follower of Jesus, or regularly considered an insider by the Western church, how can you and your group practice hospitality towards others, no matter what, even in a time of social distancing? Brainstorm ways that you can share your time and money. These ideas might be as small as keeping peanut butter and granola bars in your car to hand to homeless folks you drive by every day, or as large as organizing a fundraiser for organizations focused on justice in America. Write the list down and regularly refer to it to encourage your progress and hold yourself accountable.

2. As you know, spiritual practice consists of more than simply prayer and attending church on Sundays. If you find that you regularly attend services but do not incorporate your spiritual practice into your everyday life, consider other modes of encountering the Divine, and of sharing love and support with your local communities. One way to form relationships outside of church is through the world of art. Find art galleries in your city or town that serve as connectors in the community for people of color. Consider supporting and attending Black, Latinx, and Asian theater groups. In Luu's own hometown of Houston, there is an incredibly diverse arts and culture scene. But it is often the case that theaters owned and operated by Black artists are attended by mostly POC folks. What would it look like to make a point to seek out performances by people of color, gallery openings of artists of color, and readings and book launches featuring QTPOC? Even small steps to get out of your comfort zone could deepen and expand your engagement with your own community, your town, and the broader world over time. How could you invite others in your social circle or media following to pursue these events as well?

3. Likewise, developing your spiritual practice includes diversifying your reading list to incorporate works that aren't purely theological in nature. Consider including works of fiction, creative nonfiction, memoir, and poetry as an act of spiritual empathy. Our brains are wired for connection, and stories are how we connect to one another. For example, Austin Channing Brown's memoir—*I'm Still Here: Black Dignity in a World Made for Whiteness*—recounts her experience as a Black, Christian woman living in middle-class white America. Why not reach out to a friend, choose a work from the resources list below, and make it a point to discuss how the work has encouraged you to

engage with the world differently?

4. Wade into the waters of political discussions with your friends—away from social media. Practice listening. Share your own experiences, as we are encouraged to do in this discussion guide, by beginning from a place of curiosity and loving kindness. Start statements with phrases such as "I've come to realize" or "I find this confusing," rather than "They always say this." Give examples of how you have been affected by an idea and what it might mean for you. Remember the point of discussion is to move beyond false dichotomies and seek common humanity, while being aware that not engaging in these tough conversations can mean a refusal on our parts to examine how we might be causing others pain (i.e., a false sense of colorblindness).

Resources:

1. Luu's anti-racism reading list for beginners:
    a. Nguyen, Viet Thanh. *The Sympathizer*. New York: Grove Press, 2015.
    b. Brown, Austin Channing. *I'm Still Here: Black Dignity in a World Made for Whiteness*. New York: Convergent Books, 2018.
    c. Brown, Jericho. *The Tradition*. Port Townsend, WA: Copper Canyon Press, 2019.
    d. Kendi, Ibram X. *How to be an Anti-racist*. Rev. ed. New York: One World, 2019.
    e. Anderson, Carol. *White Rage*.
    f. Alexander, Michelle. *The New Jim Crow: Mass Incarceration in an Age of Colorblindness*. New York: The New Press, 2012.
    g. Dyson, Michael Eric. *Tears We Cannot Stop: A Sermon to White America*.

    h.   Painter, Nell Irvin. *The History of White People*. New York, NY: W. W. Norton & Company, 2010.

    i.   Fleming, Crystal Marie. *How to Be Less Stupid About Race*. Boston, MA: Beacon Press, 2018.

    j.   Washington, Bryan. *Lot: Stories*. New York: Riverhead Books, 2019.

    k.   Mouton, Deborah D.E.E.P. *Newsworthy: poems.* Houston, TX: Bloomsday Literary, 2019.

    l.   Diangelo, Robin. *White Fragility: Why It's So Hard for White People to Talk About Racism*. Boston: Beacon Press, 2018.

    m.   See also the reading list for young readers included at the end of this discussion guide.

2.   Kendi, Ibram X. "What's the Difference Between a Frat and a Gang?" *The Atlantic*, March 20, 2018." https://www.theatlantic.com/politics/archive/2018/03/america-frats-and-gangs/555896/.

3.   Jones, Camara. "Allegories on Race and Racism." Filmed July 10, 2014, in Atlanta, GA. TEDxEmory video, 20:43. https://youtu.be/GNhcY6fTyBM.

4.   Rape, Abuse, and Incest National Network. "Campus Sexual Violence: Statistics." RAINN. Accessed January 8, 2020. https://www.rainn.org/statistics/campus-sexual-violence.

5.   Park, Andrew Sung. "Minjung Theology: A Korean Contextual Theology," *Indian Journal of Theology* 33, no. 4 (October–December 1984).

6.   Bass, Diana Butler. "Table of Gifts." The Work of the People video, 9:40. https://www .theworkofthepeople.com/a-table-of-gifts.

7.   Brueggemann, Walter. "The Liturgy of Abundance, the Myth of Scarcity." *Christian Century*, March 24, 1999. https://www.christiancentury.org/article/2012-01/ liturgy-abundance-myth-scarcity.

8.   Ekblad, Bob. *Reading the Bible with the Damned*. Louisville, KY:

Westminster John Knox, 2005.

9. MacIntyre, Alasdair. *Dependent Rational Animals: Why Human Beings Need the Virtues.* Rev. ed. Chicago: Open Court, 2001.

10. Middleton, J. Richard. *The Liberating Image: The* Imago Dei *in Genesis 1.* Grand Rapids: MI, Brazos Press, 2005.

11. Harper, Lisa Sharon. *The Very Good Gospel: How Everything Wrong Can Be Made Right.* Colorado Springs, CO: WaterBrook Press, 2016.

12. Hardin, Michael. "Christianity Is Changing," Patheos, September 2014. https://www .patheos.com/blogs/ christianityischanging/2014/09/the-eucharist-4/.

13. Jersak, Bradley. *A More Christlike God: A More Beautiful Gospel.* Pasadena, CA: CWRpress, 2015.

14. Beilby, James, and Paul R. Eddy, eds. *The Nature of Atonement: Four Views.* Downers Grove, IL: InterVarsity, 2006.

15. Moore, Alan, et al. *Watchmen.* DC Comics Inc., 1987.

16. Boyle, Greg. *Barking to the Choir: The Power of Radical Kinship.* Simon & Schuster, 2017.

17. Thomas Aquinas. *Summa theologiae.* Translated by Fathers of the English Dominican Province. Notre Dame, IN: English Classics, 1947.

18. Clement of Alexandria. *The Stromata.* In *Fathers of the Second Century: Hermas, Tatian, Athenagoras, Theophilus, and Clement of Alexandria.* Vol. 2 of *The Ante-Nicene Fathers,* edited by Philip Schaff. Grand Rapids, MI: Christian Classics Ethereal Library, 2004. http://www.ccel.org/ccel/schaff/anf02.

Chapter 5: Healing from the Depths of Woundedness

> "God does not do evil so that good can occur. How do I know this? If I believe in a God who is involved in people's lives, an engaged God, then why would God need to do that? To teach us something? To make a point? If that is the case, I don't really know the point" (149).
>
> "God's love is the willingness of God to suffer and be changed in suffering" (165).
>
> "Jesus' life of passive resistance does not mean he was passive or neutral about the sin and hurt in the world. Instead, he conquered sin and death through actively loving others and resisting the forces of evil. He did not return evil for evil, but confronted evil with powerful love, love that sought the best outcome for people" (169).
>
> "We can only be healed when we look upon those wounds and see the sin and violence humans have perpetrated toward the other, and when we see that is the cause of their hurt" (170).

Questions:
Chapter 5 enters into several complex theological and philosophical conversations. You may want to focus your discussion on understanding the concepts and your group's reactions or personal anecdotes, particularly if your group is not well-versed in these subjects. The philosophical bricks laid in this chapter will allow you to expand your conversations of chapter

6 and 7 to better analyze your own lives and develop action items.

1. Touch base with one another and make sure that everyone is comfortable with the theological and philosophical ideas proposed in the chapter. Consider beginning with a discussion of the penal substitutionary view of atonement, as this is the basis from which the chapter launches into a conversation of woundedness and healing. Share your reactions to Luu's analysis of this philosophy using "I" statements. If folks are struggling with the term, read Luu's omelet-making metaphor on page 145 aloud. Then use the following questions, derived from the questions that he poses throughout the chapter, to further probe your understandings and beliefs. Break into smaller groups or pairs as is useful.

   - If we interpret Jesus' death as an act of God choosing God's Son to perish, is this a behavior of love? If so, love of whom? How can you can trust a God who behaves this way?
   - Is this God—a penal substitutionary God—any different from someone who does both good and evil? If God is all-powerful and all-creative, then why does God need to do evil in order to accomplish good?
   - How does a penal substitutionary view of God influence your faith?
     - Do you feel that sin keeps God away from you, or does it keep you away from God?
     - Do you believe that punishment can bring healing?
   - Has your view of penal substitutionary atonement changed since reading the chapter? Share your thoughts with the group.

2. In order to launch in to a larger discussion regarding the impacts

of the penal substitutionary view on everyday life, begin by considering the phrase, "Everything happens for a reason," which is often used to attribute suffering to the will of God or a greater power. In this chapter, Luu connects such language to a penal substitutionary view that can ultimately invalidate the suffering, hurt, and *han* of those who are experiencing woundedness and oppression.

- Before reading the chapter, what has been your experience with the saying "everything happens for a reason" often, especially in our time of financial, cultural, emotional, and social insecurity? Does this idea offer you comfort? After reading the chapter, has your relationship to this phrase changed or remained the same? Why?
- If you prefer to not use this phrase, why is that? Has the idea that "everything happens for a reason" ever hurt you or turned you away from a community or the church?
- As a group, consider brainstorming alternative phrases or gestures for consoling another person with compassion and empathy, as a way of leap-frogging into a larger calls-to-action throughout your discussion.

3. Luu suggests that we are all God's children, but it doesn't follow that all suffering comes from God, or that God must (or does) treat us as children by "teaching us a lesson." As Luu explains, "When we put away notions that God needs to do evil so that good can come out of it, we become more compassionate and empathetic to the problems of people" (148). Indeed, in conceiving of an empathetic and even vulnerable God, we are asked to look at our own actions and to unwind the myth of redemptive violence (108).

- How does the penal substitutionary view of God and the myth of redemptive violence hurt those who are inherently disadvantaged in our society? How has it contributed to larger structures of oppression? How have these views influenced the way we treat others and their suffering throughout history, in national politics, or even in your smaller faith communities?

- Luu references historian Timothy Gorringe's thesis that the penal substitutionary view has slowly made its way into supposedly secular politics (150). How might this view now be ingrained in state-sanctioned violence? The carceral system? Who, then, becomes society's scapegoats?

- Has the penal substitutionary view of God or justice in society personally hurt you? Turned you away? How might this view emotionally discourage people from learning about Jesus?

4. Meditate upon the following: "God is someone who can and does become vulnerable to the aches and pains of love. If 'God is love,' then God is also willing to be vulnerable to pain and change. God is the possibility of forsakenness. Love, by nature, changes us, and if God is love, then God is open to the possibility of change" (165). How does moving away from a penal substitutionary concept of God to a God changed by love affect the way you might grow as an empathetic and compassionate person of faith?

5. *Concluding activity:* "Sometimes seeking peace involves healing, and sometimes it requires confronting the power and privilege of political and religious elites" (169).

- What are constructive ways you and your community can move forward in seeking out and challenging existing power structures that are standing in the way of peace and reconciliation? What would it take for you to walk along the "third road" (170)? Write your brainstorming down.

- Have each member of your group commit to at least one action from your list in the following week.

Practices:

1. *Journal prompt, before or after discussion*: Read Ursula K. Le Guin's story, "The Ones Who Walk Away from Omelas." Take notes as your read and write down your favorite or most impactful quotes. Consider the following questions in your journal once you finish:
   - In what ways does the story parallel our current political system?
   - Who, then, represents you in the story? Who do you want to be in the story?
   - What takeaways do you have from Le Guin's piece as a whole?

2. Consider consistent volunteering. How could you make space in your life for outreach with a prison ministry? Or volunteering with activist groups who help at the borders? Where are the people that have served as society's scapegoats (159-161)? How might you pave a path to welcome them into your community?

3. Historian Howard Zinn makes the following statement: "You can't be neutral on a moving train." We have the ability to confront inequities in existing power structures and the wounds they inflict. Research your local, city, state, and national government's representatives. Reach out and ask for the change you want to see in broken systems. Do research and sign petitions calling for justice for those who have been wrongly incarcerated and/or hurt by the prison-industrial system.

4. Look inward. Make a practice of reviewing your own actions. A good way to begin this exercise is to ask yourself: "Who benefits most from my words and actions?" It may be helpful to discuss with a trusted friend, as an accountability partner. In what ways have you, through your actions or inaction, harmed others? Are there amends to be made? Seek out healing ways to reconcile yourself to others whom you have hurt.

Resources:

1. Graves, Anthony. *Infinite Hope: How Wrongful Conviction, Solitary Confinement, and 12 Years on Death Row Failed to Kill My Soul.* Boston: Beacon Press, 2018.

2. Zinn, Howard. *You Can't Be Neutral on a Moving Train: A Personal History of Our Times.* Beacon Press, 2002.

3. Cone, James. *The Cross and the Lynching Tree.* Maryknoll, NY: Orbis, 2011.

4. Girard, René. *The Scapegoat.* Baltimore: The Johns Hopkins University Press, 1986. Originally published as *Le Bouc émissaire.* Paris: Grasset, 1982.

5. Williams, James G. *The Bible, Violence, and the Sacred: Liberation from the Myth of Sanctioned Violence.* New York: HarperCollins, 1995.

6. Richards, E. Randolph, and Brandon J. O'Brien, *Misreading Scripture with Western Eyes: Removing Cultural Blinders to Better Understand the Bible.* Downers Grove, IL: IVP Books, 2012.

7. Ekblad, Bob. "God Is Not to Blame: The Servant's Atoning Suffering according to the LXX of Isaiah 53." In *Stricken by God? Nonviolent Identification and the Victory of Christ,* edited by Brad Jersak and Michael Hardin, 180-204. Abbotsford, BC: Fresh Wind Press, 2007.

8. Tidball, Derek, David Hilborn, and Justin Thacker, eds. *The Atonement Debate: Papers from the London Symposium on the*

    Theology of Atonement. Grand Rapids, MI: Zondervan Academic, 2008.

9. Wink, Walter. *The Powers That Be: Theology for a New Millennium*. New York: Doubleday, 1998.

10. Nouwen, Henri. *The Return of the Prodigal Son: A Story of Homecoming*. New York: Doubleday, 1992.

11. Moltmann, Jürgen. *The Crucified God: The Cross of Christ as the Foundation and Criticism of Christian Theology*. Minneapolis: Fortress, 1993.

12. Cone, James. *The Cross and the Lynching Tree*. Maryknoll, NY: Orbis, 2011.

13. Le Guin, Ursula K. "The Ones Who Walk Away from Omelas." In *New Dimensions 3*. Edited by Robert Silverberg. Garden City, NY: Nelson Doubleday, 1973.

14. Gorringe, Timothy. *God's Just Vengeance: Crime, Violence and the Rhetoric of Salvation*. New York, NY: Cambridge University Press, 1996.

15. Calarco, Santo. "Punished 'for' or 'by' Our Sins—The Suffering Servant of Isaiah 53." *Clarion Journal of Spirituality and Justice* (October 15, 2013). https://www.clarion-journal.com/clarion_journal_of_spirit/2013/10/punished-for-or-by-our-sins-the-suffering-servant-of-isaiah-53-santo-calarco.html.   Moltmann, Jürgen. *The Crucified God: The Cross of Christ as the Foundation and Criticism of Christian Theology*. Minneapolis: Fortress, 1993.

16. Augustine. *De Trinitate*. Edited by W. J. Mountain. CCSL 50. Turnhout: Brepols, 1970.

Chapter 6: The Death of Death

66 "It is in this kind of relationship between one's own story and the story of another that we find beauty in life. This is the essence of what it means to live the fullest kind of life" (182).

"Often, the intersection of our lives with the lives of others is a way in which we work out the deep wounds and hurt in our lives, the places of shame" (183).

"God's wounds show God's vulnerability to receiving *han*, and also the continual nature of God as one of love and vulnerability to abandonment. Just as life, true life, exists in the tension between wounds and healing, and between love and abandonment, Jesus retains his scars and we are invited to touch and see them. When we touch the wounds of the risen Christ, we are given the ability to touch our own scars and to know the possibility of life for the *han*-ridden. Those who have suffered from the perpetrators of *han* will be healed. Death is not the end, and life can spring forth" (185).

"Building up requires that we creatively do something with life, a life that involves difficulty, pain, and suffering, but also joy and hope" (189).

"For sinners, Christ offers freedom to love, and therefore to be loved. For the sinned-against, he offers empowerment to choose to confront, forgive, receive vocation, celebrate blessing, grieve, create peace, and engage in all sorts of life-giving acts" (189).

99

Questions:

Today's discussion will likely be difficult for many group members, as death is never an easy subject. As always, be sensitive to one another's emotions, take as many breaks as you need, and always put one another's lived experiences first.

1. Dip your toes in the water of this discussion by getting a sense of everyone's personal beliefs regarding the afterlife.
    *   Do you believe in an afterlife?
    *   If so, what does your concept of an afterlife look like?
    *   Is your notion of an afterlife constructed by your religious tradition, personal beliefs, or something else?

2. Use the discussion of the first question to segue into the more difficult conversation of death itself. Continue to allow an open platform in which people can share their feelings regarding death.
    *   Perhaps you have personal anecdotes to share, or have experienced the death of a friend or loved one that has deeply affected you.
    *   Is death something you are afraid of? Why?

3. Luu writes that "[o]ur lives include both a final, physical end and, throughout our life, many 'deaths' which may at times be caused by sin, whether the sin is committed by us or against us. These little defeats may come in the form of the loss of a job or the end of a relationship or other perceived failures" (178). Even if you have not had experience with the "final, physical" death, you have certainly experienced one of the smaller, more frequent deaths. Individually consider what deaths or perceived failures you particularly struggle with. Are these deaths a result of sin committed by you or against you? Come back together as a full group to address the following questions.

- How have you learned to handle these smaller deaths? Do you struggle to handle them? What are possible coping tactics?
- How might "the good news" of the gospel and of Jesus' healing change the way you deal with the smaller deaths?
- If you are not a follower of Jesus, how might a focus on healing the wounded in Western Christianity impact you? How might a focus on holistic healing in general—emotional, physical, and spiritual—benefit you?

4. Luu writes that "salvation for the Eastern fathers did not mean salvation from hell, but meant healing, wholeness, and flourishing" (180).

- What do you think of this conception of salvation—does it seem effective and productive for you and your community?
- What sort of salvation do you seek? If you are not religious, what sort of wholeness or healing do you seek?
- If sin is the consequence of death, what might you change (or seek help to change) about your thinking and daily actions in order to focus on lived experiences, salvation, and eternal life rather than a distant notion of physical death?

5. For some time, a narrow view of evangelical Christianity has meant that followers proselytize to non-believers with language and admonitions that might be considered offensive to outsiders (those not heretofore welcomed into the communion of worshippers, e.g. QTPOC, those who are not followers of Jesus).

- What might a new form of outreach look like given the principles outlined in *Jesus of the East*?
- How might a theology of the sinned against, of healing

and defeating death, offer a way into Christianity for folks who do not follow Jesus—even if this is not for the purpose of converting others to Christianity, but to simply welcome them to your table and to be welcomed to theirs?

- The chapter ends with a passage in which Luu meets and befriends a Vietnam war veteran, D.F. Brown, who had serendipitously been stationed in the same province as Luu at the time of his birth (191). This chance encounter and introduction sparked a life-long friendship. How has the act of listening and being open and vulnerable to new relationships changed or broadened your own experiences of others in your life?

6. Luu writes that those who have been burdened with *han* have a difficult choice between letting the violence and anger consume them, or to be open to the path of healing. Particularly if you are struggling with *han* or a deep woundedness, what have you done to seek healing or reconciliation?

    a. Which path do you want to take? Are you ready to choose?

    b. Who are the wounded healers in your life who can help you and stand with you?

    c. Once again, ask yourself what you need for the path of healing. Remember that you do not need to rely on yourself alone. There are a variety of options available to you, including wounded healers in your own community, or professional help.

7. *Concluding activity*: When writing about the work of Lily Yeh, Luu says that "[a]t times, people need more than words to reconcile with their past" (182). Be in community together. Allow

vulnerability and an atmosphere of healing to flourish as you consider ways to reconcile with your parts, and your hurt. Some groups have enjoyed projecting images of *kintsugi* or playing soothing music as inspiration.

- Start with words. Engage in a private journal time of around 5 minutes in which you consider your own brokenness. You have considered the question of how you have been wounded, or how you have wounded others many times throughout the study guide. Now spend time considering the depth of the impact.

    - How has being wounded, or experiencing *han*, changed the way you are able to live your everyday life?

    - If you have wounded others, directly or indirectly, meditate on this impact in their lives. How has it changed you? How has it changed your heart?

- Return to the large group to discuss creative suffering and healing. What, if any, art forms or creative endeavors do you engage with—or wish to engage with—other than words to bring about healing? How does it work for you and how do you make time for this?

- With your journaling and discussion in mind, engage in 20 minutes or more of art-making with your group. Come prepared with art supplies that you enjoy using. If your group is meeting in person, perhaps you want to tack a large piece of butcher paper to the wall and work on a shared mural. If you are meeting over Zoom, everyone can create something different while enjoy one another's presence. While you are creating, consider what sort of imagery your journal and discussion brought to your mind. What does a physical manifestation of hurt and healing look like to you?

Practices:

1. *Journal Prompt:* The prompt for this chapter is geared towards seeking salvation, healing, or both. Refresh yourself on the discussion of sociologist and educator Parker Palmer around "death-dealing" and "life-giving" practices (188). Meditate in your journal on your own practices. Are your actions and treatment of others death-dealing or life-giving? Are your actions and treatment of yourself death-dealing or life-giving? How does this honesty with yourself make you feel? Pick the following questions according to what is most relevant to you. It is important to remember that most of the time, we are not purely the sinner or the sinned against—it is possible to be both.

    - If you are burdened with *han*, what death-dealing practices are you struggling against? Return to your group's discussion of the path of healing—continue to ask yourself what you need to begin or continue your healing process. Make at least 3 action items to accomplish for yourself in the following week.

    - If you feel that you are ready to be a wounded healer, how might you offer your life-giving energy to others? Who do you want to be available to and how do you want to go about forming a community of healing?

    - If you find that your actions and behaviors are death-dealing or *han*-causing, what do you need to do to seek salvation? More simply put, in what ways can you learn to love better? How can you act with justice and address the wounds you have caused? Choose 3 action items that you will aim to accomplish in the coming week to better align your actions with healing and justice.

2. Particularly if your behaviors are death-dealing, enter into conversations where listening is your only objective. Instead of seeking to fill the space between the two of you with your own beliefs, invite an open dialogue where you seek to understand the experiences of your friends in *and* outside of your faith community.

3. Expand your Christian reading list to include theologians of color and memoirs of those who have long been considered "outsiders" or "others" to the faith. Spending time reading work that doesn't confirm your beliefs, but rather challenges your point of view, can offer valuable insights to encourage empathy and allow for further exploration of your own spiritual tenets. See "Resources" below for titles to begin with.

4. There are six activities Luu points to in chapter six that he calls the "creative intersection of *han*": art, community, healing, meaning, activity, and story. Conceive of ways that you can participate in these activities to heal yourself and others. Put them into practice. Perhaps this looks like volunteering, doing something you've always dreamed of doing that is meaningful to you, sharing your personal story on paper or in person with someone who may not know it, or creating art!

Resources:

1. Several organizations offer reading lists online. Check out the list of Black theologian authors called "25 Black Theologians Who Have Grown Our Faith" on *Christianity Today*'s website.

2. Hạnh, Thích Nhất. *Living Buddha, Living Christ*. New York: Riverhead, 1997.

3. White, Rozella Haydée. *Love Big: The Power of Revolutionary Relationships to Heal the World*. Minneapolis, MN: Fortress Press,

2019.

4. Holsten, Glenn, and Daniel Traub. *The Barefoot Artist*. New York: Film Movement, 2014. 83 minutes.

   a. Available on Lily Yeh's website at BarefootArtists.org.

5. Riedelsheimer, Thomas. *Leaning into the Wind*. Netherlands: Magnolia Pictures, 2018.

6. Heath, Elaine A. *Healing the Wounds of Sexual Abuse: Reading the Bible with Survivors*. Ada, MI: Brazos Press, 2019.

7. Rambo, Shelly. *Resurrecting Wounds: Living in the Afterlife of Trauma*. Waco, TX: Baylor University Press, 2017.

8. Bolz-Weber, Nadia. *Accidental Saints: Finding God in All the Wrong People*. New York: Convergent Books, 2015.

9. Jersak, Bradley. *Her Gates Will Never Be Shut: Hope, Hell, and the New Jerusalem*. Eugene, OR: Wipf and Stock, 2009.

10. Bernstein, Alan E. *The Formation of Hell: Death and Retribution in the Ancient and Early Christian Worlds*. London: University of London Press, 2003.

11. Rohr, Richard. *Immortal Diamond: The Search for Our True Self*. San Francisco: Jossey- Bass, 2013.

12. Brant, Jo-Ann A. *John*. Paideia Commentaries on the New Testament. Grand Rapids, MI: Baker Academic, 2011.

13. Rambo, Shelly. "Wounds Surfacing." Stanley Grenz Lecture Series, Seattle, WA, November 2015. https://vimeo.com/146464773.

14. Widdicombe, Peter. "The Wounds and the Ascended Body: The Marks of Crucifixion in the Glorified Christ from Justin Martyr to John Calvin." *Laval théologique et philosophique* 59, no. 1 (February 2003): 137–54.

15. Palmer, Parker. "The Broken-Open Heart: Living with Faith and Hope in the Tragic Gap." Reprinted from *Weavings: A Journal of the Christian Spiritual Life*, vol. 24, no. 2. (March/April 2009). https://www.couragerenewal.org/PDFs/PJP-WeavingsArticle-

Broken-OpenHeart.pdf.

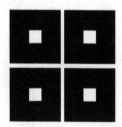

Chapter 7: The Birth of Kingdom

" "For those who suffer injustice, God is a co-conspirator, helping to move the arc of history toward justice. Joining God in achieving this justice is a long and arduous work, helped by that for which the cosmos longs" (203).

"Jesus is victorious over justice not because he rules with the sword, but because the sword does not rule him" (208).

"Because God contains diversity within God's very self, this understanding of God reflects a community with God characterized by unity of differences and unity in differences. It is in this kind of community that healing can occur" (222).

"Those who are citizens of this kingdom seek to create spaces where the *han*-ridden can find both healing for their wounds and comfort in one another. They seek to help people engage in acts of forgiveness and find solutions that restore others to be the persons they were created to be, in the image of God. The territory of the kingdom appears in places that might not even seem religious in nature, but that reveal God's intent for the world, spaces where sinners and the sinned-against meet. These are the places that Christ inhabits, the places of *han*" (230). "

Questions:

1. Briefly review the major concepts related to justice that Luu outlines throughout the chapter: reconciliation (199), justice (201), retributive justice (206), restorative justice (210), and distributive justice (213). Hold space for an open platform in which folks can discuss their feelings towards, and reactions to,

the various types of justice and reconciliation. What appealed to you? What was new to you? And as always, for those individuals or groups that are *han*-afflicted, allow space for the pain and joy of memories (both hurt and healing). Allow space for rage and hope and personal experience.

2. Consider your introductory conversation about reconciliation and justice. In Chapter 7, Luu writes: "When humans do nothing to work at sowing peace in this world, then the reconciliation work of God cannot be accomplished. Justice work must be at the center. . . For those who suffer injustice, God is a co-conspirator, helping to move the arc of history toward justice" (201-203). Racist systems must be dismantled. Peace can be prayed for, but must also be acted into being. Every choice we make is an action, either towards justice or not. Allow space to be self-critical in order to open up further conversation. These questions can be answered as a large group, in pairs, or privately in your journal.

   - What tenets do you hold in your heart when you vote?
   - Are you critical about the way you consume and fact check political and social information? Do you know how to avoid confirmation bias and to avoid being a victim of harmful propaganda?
   - How do you make choices on where and how you spend your money?
   - How do your choices influence systems of injustice; how do systems of injustice, in turn, influence your choices?

3. Based on your answers to the previous question, what part do you play in the act of reconciliation regarding marginalized populations in America? Remember that for those who don't have access to even basic necessities, and for those who "are the targets of daily oppression, the 'not yet' is too far away" (199).

- In what spaces are you learning more about equity and justice?
- How can you center ideas and actions of justice in your life?
- Particularly if you are a follower of Jesus, consider the two paragraphs at the bottom of page 202, beginning with the sentence, "At the heart of the gospel is justice." As Luu explains, social and restorative justice are deeply wound into the fabric of the Christian faith. What does an active, justice-oriented faith look like to you?

4. The title of this chapter, "Birth of a Kingdom," carries a significant weight. Like Nate Parker, and to some extent Spike Lee, Luu has repurposed the title of the film *Birth of a Nation* to bring us face-to-face with issues of reconciliation. For some time, Western concepts of Jesus have focused on reconciling oneself to God as individuals, prizing "private and individual relationships with God over social and societal change" (204). But as Luu argues, salvation is not about a punitive God reconciling with humans, it's about humans doing the hard work, the real work of reconciling with others—in this way, we can come to more fully know God. What can God's people do now to turn away from the individual's own atonement and towards a fuller reconciliation of God's people?

- If you have developed greater understanding throughout this discussion process or done more research you may want to return to the following question that was posed earlier in the guide: consider your personal communities, geographic communities, and political communities. Who is committing violence and perpetrating *han*? How must they be held accountable?
- How can you ensure that your church or faith community

is not a haven in which the infliction of *han* occurs, unchecked?

5. "Walk into the darkness and hold it in your hands," says artist, Lily Yeh. In a film documenting her quest to follow her artistic passions and to bring about her family's restoration, she advocates that understanding brokenness—holding it in your hands—is the only way to create something new, something better.

   • How does this apply to the call to birth a new kingdom?
   • How will you join in the restoration of all creation?
   • Share your reactions to the idea of *dan*. What does its implementation look like in your own life or communities?

6. What questions do you still have after finishing the book that you would like to pursue either through your own research, or by following the Practices provided throughout this guide and turning to the Resource materials? If you were to have a conversation with an Eastern father, what would you continue to have questions about? What would you ask?

7. *Concluding activity:* Finally, after finishing *Jesus of the East*, what actions/behaviors have you identified in yourself that you might work to change as you move forward in community with others?

   • Particularly for those who have been sinned against and who are afflicted by *han*, consider what restorative justice looks like to you.
   • What do you think about Luu's argument regarding *dan*, or the choice of the *han*-afflicted to follow the path of anger and hurt, or that of forgiveness and reparation. Are you ready or able to forgive those who have sinned against you at this point in time? Is this a step you are

willing or even able to take?

- Consider the idea of the sentencing circle Luu describes on pages 211-12. Would you be open to trying this as a community or in your personal life? If you would find it helpful, consider drafting a plan as a group.

- Throughout this extended study, you have begun to create a healing plan and/or a restorative plan of salvation for yourself. Now is the time to share the beginnings of your journal and plan. Trade ideas, and encourage one another.

  - What, as a whole community, do you need for holistic healing? How might you hold one another accountable?

  - Your group can create their own Venn diagrams representing communities of healing—place your own names in the Venn diagram to better understand where you are in relation to one another, and thus how you can work together going forward.

  - What sort of continued study or practice can your group conduct even beyond the final page of the book?

Practices:

1. *Ongoing journal practice:* Begin a personal action/justice work inventory that you return to weekly or even daily. This practice is not intended to be shared with others. You are not doing this to "prove" anything. Instead it is a promise of accountability that you are making to yourself. Questions to ask yourself:

   - How many minutes a day do you spend talking? How many minutes a day do you spend just listening?

   - When was the last time someone challenged your ideas by sharing their own lived experiences? Who challenged you? Someone who does or doesn't look like you? How did you respond to that challenge?

- How have you done equity/social justice work that isn't simply sharing posts on social media?

- What have you done in the past week to practice reparations through the donation of emotional, monetary, or physical energy?

2. If you frequently recite the Lord's daily prayer, slow down or stop to truly consider the words. Study the meaning line-by-line, as you would annotate a poem. Use the chart on page 217 to guide you.

3. Watch the documentary of artist Lily Yeh detailing her life and life's work, *The Barefoot Artist*. (The film is available through her website at BarefootArtists.org.) First and foremost, be inspired! What changes will you make in your life, the life of your family, the lives of others, to restore creation?

Resources:

1. Yeh, Lily. "From Broken to Whole: Lily Yeh at TedXCornell U." Published December 20, 2013. TedXCornell U video, 22:23. https://www.youtube.com/watch?v=fVCXF6PN0g4

2. Lee, Spike, director. *BlacKkKlansman*. Focus Features, 2018.

3. Boyle, Gregory. *Tattoos on the Heart: The Power of Boundless Compassion*. New York: Free Press, 2010.

4. U.S. Department of Justice. "Sentencing Circles." n.d. http://www.courts.ca.gov/ documents/SentencingCircles.pdf.

5. Westervelt, Eric. "An Alternative to Suspension and Expulsion: 'Circle Up!' " NPR, December 17, 2014. https://www.npr.org/sections/ed/2014/12/17/347383068/ an-alternative-to-

suspension-and-expulsion-circle-up.

6. Langman, Peter. "Statistics on Bullying and School Shootings." School Shooters, November 2014. https://schoolshooters.info/sites/default/files/bullying_school_ shootings_1.1.pdf.

7. Grabow, Chip, and Lisa Rose. "The US Has Had 57 Times as Many School Shootings as the Other Major Industrialized Nations Combined." CNN, May 21, 2018. https://www.cnn.com/2018/05/21/us/school-shooting-us-versus-world-trnd/index.html.

8. Franco, Aaron, and Morgan Radford. "Ex-KKK Member Denounces Hate Groups One Year after Rallying in Charlottesville." NBC News, August 9, 2018. https://www.nbcnews.com/news/us-news/ex-kkk-member-denounces-hate-groups-one-year-after-rallying-n899326.

9. Cole, Nicki Lisa. "9 Surprising Facts About Welfare Recipients." ThoughtCo, updated September 28, 2019. https://www.thoughtco.com/who-really-receives-welfare- 4126592.

10. Kornfield, Jack. *The Art of Forgiveness, Lovingkindness, and Peace*. New York: Bantam, 2002.

11. De La Torre, Miguel A. *Embracing Hopelessness*. Minneapolis: Fortress, 2017.

12. Bulatao, R. A., and N.B. Anderson, eds. *Understanding Racial and Ethnic Differences in Health in Late Life: A Research Agenda*. Washington, DC: National Academies Press, 2004. https://www.ncbi.nlm.nih.gov/books/NBK24685/.

13. Bui, Anthony L., Matthew M. Coates, and Ellicott C. Matthay. "Years of Life Lost due to Encounters with Law Enforcement in the USA, 2015–2016." *Journal of Epidemiology and Community Health* 72 (2018): 715–18.

14. Perkins, John M. *Dream with Me: Race, Love, and the Struggle We Must Win*. Grand Rapids, MI: Baker Books, 2017.

15. *Christianity Today* editors. "John MacArthur's 'Statement on

Social Justice' Is Aggravating Evangelicals: Christians Are Talking Past Each Other Once Again. What's Going On?" *Christianity Today*, September 12, 2018. https://www .christianitytoday.com/ct/2018/september-web-only/john-macarthur-statement-social-justice-gospel-thabiti.html.

16. Volf, Miroslav. *Exclusion and Embrace: A Theological Exploration of Identity, Otherness, and Reconciliation*. Nashville: Abingdon, 1996.

17. Boring, Eugene. *Revelation*. Interpretation: A Bible Commentary for Preaching and Teaching 43. Knoxville, TN: Westminster John Knox, 2011.

18. Flood, Derek. "Substitutionary Atonement and the Church Fathers: A Reply to the Authors of *Pierced for Our Transgressions*." *Evangelical Quarterly* 82, no. 2 (2010): 142–159.

19. Rasmussen, Larry. *Earth-Honoring Faith: Religious Ethics in a New Key*. New York: Oxford University Press, 2013.

20. Bonhoeffer, Dietrich. *Letters and Papers from Prison*. New York: Touchstone, 1953.

Additional Reading Resources for Young Children:

Coretta Scott King Book Award Honorees
These awards are given annually to outstanding African American authors and illustrators of books for children and young adults that demonstrate an appreciation of African American culture and universal human values.

- *The Undefeated* written by Kwame Alexander and illustrated by Kadir Nelson, age 6+
- *New Kid* by Jerry Craft, age 8+
- *Sulwe* written by Lupita Nyong'o and illustrated by Vashti Harrison, age 4+
- *What is Given from the Heart* written by Patricia McKissack and illustrated by April Harrison
- Find more at http://www.ala.org/rt/emiert/cskbookawards

Other Recommendations

- *Hidden Figures: The True Story of Four Black Women and the Space Race* by Margot Lee Shetterly
- *Monday's Not Coming* by Tiffany D. Jackson
- *Your Kids Aren't Too Young to Learn About Race: Resource Roundup* by Katrina Michie on https://www.prettygooddesign.org/
- Visit commonsensemedia.org for an extensive list of literary resources about race for young people.

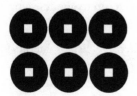

On Writing *Jesus of the East*: A Conversation with Phuc Luu and Kate Martin Williams

This an edited version of the conversation that took place at the virtual launch of Luu's book. You can watch the entire event at phucluu.com/faqs.

Kate: Can we talk about the structure of the book, because I think it's a lovely point of entry for our listeners who haven't read it yet. There are three things you do in this book: You lay out a re-conceiving of Jesus by taking us through the evolution of a Western view of Jesus (which is no small task), and explain where things might have been different had church leaders chosen differently. But right up against that, you bring readers immediately into the present with your own experience as an immigrant from Vietnam. You share stories of leaving, moving around the US, and of visiting Vietnam again: visiting the tunnels, the tangled web of wires that is the past and present in Hanoi. And there are also vignettes where you place the readers in the intimate moments of the historical Jesus. Talk to me about these threads all existing in you, and what led you to start knitting them together for this book.

Phuc: Well, I was crocheting (*says jokingly*). No, I thought about the history of this country—where we are and how we got here—and wanted to answer the question as a theologian first, but then also through my own story. I know I could not tell the story of this nation, a story of racial strife, harm done against others, especially Black and brown bodies, without also telling the story of Christianity and its origins: how Christianity started as a religion of peace and one whose members were also persecuted and killed, whose savior was persecuted and killed. In the United States, we've not inherited that story but a much different story of a colonized Christianity and a conquered Christianity. Where my story comes into play is that I was and am a product of that conquered and conquering

Christianity. My parents, brother, and I came here because of the Vietnam War, the American War. Vietnam had been the target of many attempted conquests and invasions. So the intersections of my story, the Christ story, and the American story show up in this book.

Kate: It's such a compelling structure. It's accessible. [For] scholars, lay people, sinners, sinned Against, Christians and non-Christians. The book is doing the thing you're saying Jesus calls us to do, which is expand love, [and] seek more knowledge, not less.

I re-read your chapter 4—which is about race—the night the Black Lives Matter protests began all over the US. The chapter is called "God Against the Machine" and is preceded by a single page with the definition of the Korean concept of *han* (which you point out is nearly untranslatable) and means something like or near "the deep wounded suffering of a people." This book is not just about Jesus, it's, quite simply, about healing *han*. Can you talk more about how you see that *han* can be healed? And whose job is it?

Phuc: Yes, *han* is the experience of deep woundedness. It is a word with Chinese origins, but finds its way to the Korea because of the many conquests, including a Japanese invasion and a civil war. Vietnamese has a related word to *han*, *oán hận*. Vietnam has a history of fighting off the conquest by the Chinese, Japanese, and French, and in many ways, the Americans. So, there is a deep woundedness that these countries share.

In the United States, the closest thing we have is "the blues." Where did the blues come from? Of course, a history of slavery and oppression. Here we have the opportunity to start the healing of *han*. For Black people in America, it means coming together to find healing and solidarity. Black Americans cannot wait for white people to offer them healing and restitution. We need to protest. We need to speak truth to power. But we need to know that giving ourselves space for healing and restoration are also acts of resistance. The other side of *han* is *dan*. This means to "cut off" to say "no," to resist. This can be healing in itself. We have the ability to resist the continual hurt. Now is the time to do it.

So, in different ways, we all have the responsibility to bring healing. The perpetrators need to change their minds and attitudes, therefore their actions. The victims must give themselves space to be healed. African slaves gathered together in what is called "hush arbors" where later churches were built. These spaces were where Black people could come together is find comfort and healing in the gospel.

Kate: One of the tenets, or as our friend Jess called it, tent poles, of *han* is the idea of scarcity. Our problems with the construct of race stem from this idea of scarcity. Can you get into that now? Particularly how scarcity leads to the outsized consequences of racism running unchecked in the ranks of our police structure.

Additionally, the subtitle of Jesus of the East is "Reclaiming the Gospel for the Wounded"—what the subtitle says is that the emphasis moves from the sinner (and the sinner's forgiveness) to the sinned against. When we first talked about your concept for this book—it was such an awakening for me. That yeah, Christians could stand to move the "atomized lens" as you call it, off the individual sinner, and shift focus. What does a Christianity look like if we shifted the lens to the sinned against?

Phuc: Well that would be an entirely different project, as Walter Brueggemann would say. It means that we no longer offer cheap grace to the sinner, but also work to restore the sinned against. It would mean that we spend time looking at our system of scarcity, how we don't all value the image of God in others. This nation is built on a value gap: some lives are [deemed as] worth more than others. We see this on a social and economic level. We know where Black and brown bodies fall into that gap.

In order to have justice and peace for all, we have to start with the ones who don't have it. We can't say "blue lives matter" or "all lives matter," because we are officiating the fact that Black and brown lives don't matter here in the United States. Until the unlawful policing of Black bodies stop and the illegal detaining of brown bodies who seek asylum ceases, we will continue to exist as a nation giving a pass to the wrong-doers and continually hurting the victims. Violence is then the only consequence.

Kate: I wanted to talk to you about the section in Chapter 4 about Jesus and politics, on p.117. The question is: what then do we do with this today? What do you say to someone who is Christian and claims to not want to get into politics?

Phuc: Politics involves participating in the good of the town or city. That's what the word means, *polis* or city. Jesus always spoke about the city, either against his government of Rome or the policies of the Pharisees, or how people treated others within his own community. He placed this critique against his vision of an alternative city or government, one that was open and inclusive, life giving and abundant. When Jesus said "kingdom of God," he was being political. That would be like me saying, "I believe in a vision of government other than the American one." How radical and unpatriotic is that? But many Americans believe that the United States already created the kingdom of God in their founding of this government, that somehow the founding fathers were Christians and that this is a Christian nation. This nation is far from that.

Kate: I was struck by this in chapter 7, near the end of the book. You write: "For those who suffer injustice, God is a co-conspirator, helping to move the arc of history toward justice." Can you maybe first provide some context for us about God as co-conspirator?

Phuc: Yes, the arc of history part is from MLK, but the idea of God being a co-conspirator is one in which Jesus is on the side of the wounded. He stands with the those who suffer and participates in the bending of this arc. You see, Jesus shows us that God is not like a master puppeteer or chess master, moving all the pieces and manipulating history. God is co-creator, co-laborer, working with us. But we must be also doing the work.

The word "con-spirator" comes from the Latin words meaning "to breathe with." God breathes with us when we cannot breathe. God was the one who died from hanging and suffocation. Jesus gives us the Sprit so that we can continue to breathe and do the work of bringing justice to this world. Not punitive, but restorative justice. God, not being able to breathe, dying on the lynching tree, is also the one who will give us breath to continue. We need to work together with others and with God in doing this work. This will be one of the topics of my next book, *Spirit of the East.*

Acknowledgements from Phuc

I am tremendously grateful for the outpouring of support and interest in *Jesus of the East: Reclaiming the Gospel for the Wounded*. Like many authors who had book launches during the pandemic, I dreaded not being able to be physically present with people to shake hands, give a warm embrace, and personally thank. But through the miracle of technology, people who might not have been able to easily travel to Houston showed up and filled my heart with joy. I am very thankful to be able to write, create, give expression in this time when all these things are so much more difficult to do so.

Herald Press continues to do great work with authors even in the midst of difficult times. Purchasing books from independent publishers and bookstores continues the work of putting good, no, excellent books in the hands of hungry readers.

Kate Martin Williams and Jessica Cole were very generous with their time and writing skills in pulling together this work. They brought this work across the finish line when my teaching, writing, and research schedules were almost too much to handle. I am also grateful to my publicity assistant, Lily Wulfemeyer who worked diligently to connect with book groups and individuals to make these readings and interactions happen. Lily also added much needed resources and perspective to this work.

Glossary of Terms

BIPOC

An acronym standing for Black, Indigenous, and People of Color used to describe those who are not white. Even though there might be overlap in the description, it helps to call differences in the experiences of each group.

catadores

The name for garbage pickers in Brazil; those who make their subsistence by picking through trash. This has become an occupation not only in South America, but also in Africa and Asia. The latter is the destination for much of the garbage (hundreds of millions of tons) that is shipped from the United States to be recycled. Even though the trash provides the benefit of wages, harm comes in the form of child labor and occupational health risks.

Cartesian

Refers to René Descartes, the 17th century philosopher whose *Mediations on First Philosophy* (Meditationes de Prima Philosophia) greatly influenced the Western world, especially in the sciences. His attempts to bridge science and religion ended up creating a greater divide.

dan 단

A word borrowed from the Chinese 斷, this Korean term that means "to cut off." *Dan* is an alternative strategy to *han* in which the oppressed practice self-denial and resistance to revenge and violence against their oppressors in order to prevent further hurt and end the cycle of sin.

enfleshment

> The incarnation, the entering of God into the world in the form of a person. This challenges the mind/body, spiritual/material distinction that is found in ancient Gnosticism and modern Cartesian philosophy, which question the goodness of the body.

ethics

> Simply put, the study of the good and how we pursue it.

Gnostic / Gnosticism

> Specific religious sects/members of the 1st century BCE–2nd century CE who believed in the separation between the material and the spiritual, seeing matter to be evil and spiritual to be good. Because of this dichotomy, they valued secret knowledge as an escape from the confines of the material world.

***han* 한**

> An almost untranslatable word used to describe the deep woundedness of the Korean people. *Han* is a sense of unresolved victimization that can lead to anger, hatred, and violence. *Han* is a loanword from Chinese (恨) and is related to the Vietnamese words *hận* and *oán hận*, translated as "hatred" and "animus," respectively.

imago Dei

> A Latin term that means "image of God," taken from Genesis 1:27. The Eastern Fathers believed that all humans were created in this image, but distinguished it from the "likeness of God." Whereas the former is natural to all humans, the latter is developed through discipleship with God.

kintsugi

Japanese term meaning "golden seams," which is related to the Japanese aesthetic of imperfection called *wabi-sabi* (roughly translated as "irregularly-aged").

Minjung 민중신학

Korean word referring to the people's theology: *ochlos*, ὄχλος (Greek), crowds, multitude, people, those to whom Jesus ministered, the sick, the poor, the prostitutes, the tax collectors, the shunned, the oppressed, the sinned-against. The term emerged from the experience of Christians in South Korea.

QTPOC

Acronym standing for queer/trans people of color.

racism

As defined by Camara Jones, "a system of structuring opportunity and assigning value based on the social interpretation of how one looks."

recapitulation

A Greco-Roman rhetorical term meaning to sum up the main points of an argument (Greek ἀνακεφαλαίωσις; Latin *recirculatio*). In Latin, the term *caput* refers to the head or the chapter (of a book), so the idea of recapitulation is that Jesus summed up the life of Adam through his own life. Jesus is the "second Adam" who fulfilled a life of intimacy with God, whereas Adam rejected this kind of relationship with God and instead sought the power of the knowledge of the tree of good and evil. See Ephesians 1:10. Irenaeus of Lyons uses this term to talk about the redemption of humans by Jesus.

theosis

> The idea presented by the Eastern fathers that humans can grow into the likeness of God. This is also known as divinization, in which people are restored to their original human nature and become united to the divine. In the early Eastern church this was expressed through Athanasius's famous statement, "The Word of God became human so that humans can become more like God."

thầy

> A Vietnamese term meaning "teacher." The equivalent to the Hebrew "rabbi" or Greek "dáskalos" (δάσκαλος) or the Latin "magister."

theology

> The study of how humans interpret their relationship to the divine. Literally, "conversation with God."

YHWH

> The tetragrammaton or the four-letter name of God represented by the for Hebrew letters, יהוה.

việt kiều 粵僑

> An inbetweener, foreign-born Vietnamese, part of the diaspora after the Vietnam War (the American War) ended in 1975. There are 4.5 million "overseas Vietnamese," or "Vietnamese sojourners," who sought political and economic asylum.

Authors

Phuc Luu (福 刘) immigrated with his family to the United States from Vietnam when he was four. Luu is now a theologian, philosopher, and artist creating work in Houston, Texas, to narrow the divide between ideas and beauty. If theology is speaking about God, Luu seeks to give new language and grammar to what theology has not yet said. He served for seven years on the Nobel Peace Prize Committee for the American Friends Service Committee (Quakers). He holds degrees in theology (MDiv, PhD) and philosophy (MA), but has learned the most from the places where people ask difficult questions, where they live in the land between pain and hope, and where these stories are told.

Kate Martin Williams is a cofounder at Bloomsday. She attended the University of Tennessee and earned a Master of Arts in English with a Creative Writing emphasis. In addition, Kate holds a Master of Arts in Teaching from Rice University.

Jessica Cole is an editor/co-owner of Bloomsday Literary. She has a masters in English from UC Davis, where she wrote a thesis in poetry, and a PhD in English from the University of Tennessee. The novel she wrote for her dissertation re-imagines a chapter in scientific history.

Lily Wulfemeyer is a freelance literary marketing agent and editor, as well as a writer working on their first hybrid collection of short stories and poems. In the last few years, they've worked as a literary magazine editor, student art show curator, newspaper article writer, and production assistant for a podcast. They graduated from Rice University with a degree in English and a minor in Museums and Cultural Heritage, with a Distinction in Creative Work.

CPSIA information can be obtained
at www.ICGtesting.com
Printed in the USA
LVHW040219161120
671798LV00006B/668

9 780578 795720